SUMMARY

&ANALYSIS

OF

Measure

What

Matters

*How Google, Bono, and the Gates Foundation
Rock the World with OKRs*

A GUIDE TO THE BOOK
BY JOHN DOERR

ᵦᵧ ZIPREADS

NOTE: This book is a summary and analysis and is meant as a companion to, not a replacement for, the original book.
Please follow this link to purchase a copy of the original book: https://amzn.to/2DccFMz

TABLE OF CONTENTS

SYNOPSIS

In his book *Measure What Matters,* John Doerr develops a practical methodology for realizing the true potential of an organization.

The core concept is that of Objectives and Key Results associated with each objective. An objective is the "what" is to be achieved, while the key objectives are "how" this will be accomplished. These so-called OKRs provide a framework for pushing all employees from the CEO to the frontline worker to greater heights by aligning all goals so that they contribute to the organization's mission.

To work, OKRs must be transparent, and they should flow both from the top-down, and from the bottom-up. Sometimes, the culture of the company must evolve before OKRs can function productively.

Working hand in hand with OKRs are CFRs, standing for Conversation, Feedback, and Recognition. Together, they can be combined to raise organizations and their employees even higher.

Doerr provides many high-profile examples of where OKRs have been implemented to great effect, including the Gates Foundation and Google. However, it may be the lesser-known organizations that resonate more with a particular reader since they may align better with their business model and/or goals.

Either way, *Measure What Matters* provides an entertaining exploration of how these seemingly simple concepts could revolutionize your organization.

PART 1: OKRS IN ACTION

GOOGLE, MEET OKRS

Doerr introduces the concept of Objectives and Key Results (OKRs) by relaying the story of his first meeting with the founders of Google, Larry Page and Sergey Brin. In his presentation to their company in 1999, he explained that his objective that day was to build a planning model for their company, which would be measured by three key results: (1) He would finish his presentation on time; (2) He would create a sample set of quarterly Google OKRs; and (3) He would gain agreement from Google management for a three-month OKR trial.

Key Takeaway: Ideas are easy. Execution is everything.

The results from that meeting were nothing short of spectacular. Larry Page wrote the Foreword for Doerr's book, giving a lot of credit for Google's huge success to the principles of OKRs. Eric Smidt too, credited OKRs with "changing the course of the company forever." (Doerr, p. 14). Doerr introduces several other key examples, including "Operation Crush," to which we return in Chapter 3.

The concept of OKRs, not surprisingly, is based on two key ideas: (1) Objectives; and (2) Key Results.

Key Takeaway: An Objective is WHAT is to be achieved.

Objectives should be significant and action-oriented. Ideally, they should be inspiring.

Key Takeaway: Key results are HOW you get the objective done.

Key results must be measurable, specific, verifiable, and aggressive. But they should also be achievable within some articulable time span.

A complementary concept to the OKR is the CFR, standing for Conversation, Feedback, and Recognition. We explain CFRs in more detail in Chapter 15.

OKRs also facilitate flatter organizational charts. Whereas conventional wisdom suggests a "rule of seven," allowing a maximum of seven direct reports to each manager, some of Google's managers would have more than 20, leading to less oversight and more autonomy by employees, which, in turn produces more breakthroughs.

THE FATHER OF OKRS

The originator of the concept of OKRs can be traced back to Andy Grove, the so-called "Father of OKRs." Grove was a Hungarian refugee who had escaped from the Nazis and moved to the U.S. at the age of 21. He was penniless, spoke little English, and had severe hearing loss. Grove led Intel to be the dominant player in the microprocessor market.

According to Grove: "The two key phrases . . . are objectives and the key result. And they match the two purposes. The objective is the direction: 'We want to dominate the mid-range microcomputer component business.' That's an objective. That's where we're going to go. Key results for this quarter: 'Win ten new designs for the 8085' is one key result. It's a milestone. The two are not the same. . . The key result has to be measurable. But at the end you can look, and without any arguments: Did I do that or did I not do it? Yes? No? Simple. No judgments in it." (Doerr, p. 22).

This philosophy led them to dominate the mid-range microcomputer business.

Key Takeaway: Healthy OKR culture should include a ruthless intellectual honesty, no self-interest, and strong ties with the team.

Grove transformed the industry standard concept of "Management by Objectives" or MBOs (which he labeled iMBOs. The "what" became "what" and "how." The annual time frame became quarterly or monthly. MBOs were no longer private but were public and transparent. Rather than being top-down, they were bottom-up, or sideways. Generally, they were not tied to compensation as they had been in the past. And finally, they were not risk averse, but aggressive and aspirational.

OPERATION CRUSH: AN INTEL STORY

Operation Crush was the name given to a famous fight for survival by the then young Intel Corporation, and provides our first example of OKRs in action.

In late 1979, Intel realized that they were at war with Motorola who had been producing high-performance microprocessors that were faster and easier to program than Intel's. Thus, began the campaign, known as Operation Crush, to restore Intel back to its position as a market leader.

Key Takeaway: OKR Superpowers are focus, alignment, tracking, and stretching.

Remarkably, none of Intel's products were changed for Operation Crush. Instead, Grove and his team adapted their marketing strategy to emphasize their strengths. OKRs played a key role. They allowed the operation to permeate through the ranks almost immediately. With an initial meeting attended by 100 people, the message propagated through three levels within 24 hours. "Fiefdoms" were sacrificed, and all objectives were aligned with the common goal. The goliath Motorola could not respond in time to this change in tactics. By 1986, Intel had reclaimed 85 percent of the 16-bit microprocessor market, and today, tens of billions of Intel microcontrollers are embedded within everything from computers to centrifuges.

"Bad companies are destroyed by crisis. Good companies survive them. Great companies are improved by them" – Andy Grove (Doerr, p. 44).

SUPERPOWER #1: FOCUS AND COMMIT TO PRIORITIES

To be effective, OKRs require that you answer basic questions like: What are most important objectives for the next three months? This list should include only a handful of key objectives. Google, for example, used its mission statement to "Organize the world's information and make it universally accessible and useful." From this came a range of carefully thought out products, including Android, Chrome, and Google Earth. However, in addition to communicating "what" must be done, leaders must also communicate "why."

Key Takeaway: "Innovation means saying no to one thousand things." – Steve Jobs

Key results, particularly when the OKR is more ambitious should be paired. By creating both a "quality" and "quantity" goal, potentially flawed OKRs can be avoided. The case of the Ford Pinto provides an illuminating illustration. Due to aggressive demands from Ford's CEO, safety checks in the planning and development stages of the car's development were overlooked. In particular, the gas tank was placed too close to the rear bumper. Crash tests demonstrated that a one-dollar piece of plastic would have stopped the puncture of the tank, but the solution was discarded because of the extra cost and weight. Ford had defined clear objectives and goals, but one of the goals lacking was safety (a quality goal). Thus, pairing a quantity goal, such as $50M in Q1 sales with $10M in Q1 maintenance contracts, for example, will ensure that new customers will also be satisfied customers.

Ground rules for setting your key results include making them succinct, specific, and measurable. Also, paraphrasing Voltaire, do not allow the perfect to be the enemy of the good. Finally, remember that less is often more. As Grove said: "Keep the number of objectives small . . . Each time you make a commitment, you forfeit your chance to commit to something else" (Doerr, p. 56).

FOCUS: THE REMIND STORY

Brett Kopf, cofounder of Remind explains how OKRs helped his young company focus on identifying the right goals to create a "Twitter for education." Inspired by his own failures in high school and college, he asked why teachers couldn't connect directly with their students using their smartphones? With his brother, David, his solution was to create an app, but the journey was difficult and they narrowly avoided bankruptcy. However, OKRs gave them a way to focus on the key objectives they needed to achieve their ultimate goal.

Key Takeaway: Focus is essential to be able to choose the right goals.

Brett gives an example of an often-requested feature: the repeated message. A teacher wants to remind her class to bring a particular book to school, and automatically send out that reminder every Monday, say. Using OKRs, they evaluated its ability to improve user engagement with the engineering effort required to implement it. They concluded that it was not a high enough priority, despite its "delight" appeal.

For Brett, OKRs also helped with his personal focus. He limited his individual objectives to three or four. And, using OKRs, Brett and David have remained true to their vision: "to give every student an opportunity to succeed."

COMMIT: THE NUNA STORY

Jini Kim, cofounder and CEO of Nuna tells how she was inspired to create a new Medicaid data platform from scratch because of her autistic brother.

Kim had joined Google in 2004, working with the Google Health platform. Realizing how difficult it was to gain access to health care data, she formed Nuna in 2010. Although relatively successful, it was not until 2015 when she implemented OKRs, based on her experience at Google, that things really began to take off.

Key Takeaway: OKRs require both strength and commitment.

Yet, the path remained difficult. Some people never set their own OKRs, while others set them, but then file them away. Jini says that with hindsight, she would have approached OKRs differently. For example, she would have limited the concept to her leadership team of five, not everybody at Nuna.

In spite of these growing pains, OKRs helped Nuna deliver on its objectives. In January 2017, the acting director of the Centers for Medicare and Medicaid Services described Nuna's cloud database as "near historic" in the *New York Times*.

SUPERPOWER #2: ALIGN AND CONNECT FOR TEAMWORK

In spite of transparency being the default mode for many aspects of our lives (e.g., Facebook, Twitter, and Instagram), within the business community goals often remain secret.

Traditionally, goals are set at the top by executives. These trickle down to lower-level officers, and on to employees, with each lower-level goal being a key result from the boss' set of objectives. One of the problems with this is that alignment between the goals and objectives is rare. Moreover, it takes a substantial amount of time to create all of these cascading goals, and they often result in marginalized contributors, particularly at the lowest levels.

In contrast, by using OKRs, which are, by definition, transparent, everyone from the newest employee to the CEO can see everyone else's goals and expected results. This allows people to comment on and assist others in achieving their goals. And, even more importantly, frees up people to contribute "up the chain" by defining their own OKRs that they know are in alignment with some greater company strategy.

Key Takeaway: Combine a bottoms-up approach to goal setting with the traditional top-down approach to achieve your goals.

Many examples of this philosophy exist, but perhaps the best one is the so-called "20 percent time" that Google provides their employees. Free to work on their own projects, they can strive to create something new and novel that contributes to the over-arching objectives of the company. This was, for example, how Gmail was conceived and developed. Now it is the most popular email system in the world.

ALIGN: THE MYFITNESSPAL STORY

Mike Lee conceived of MyFitnessPal while getting ready for his wedding. He had wanted to lose some weight and consulted with a fitness trainer. He received a list of food and a paper document for tracking calories. As a programmer, he knew there must be a better way. Teaming up with his brother, Albert, the two created MyFitnessPal.

Early on, a key OKR for the company was defined by the objective: Help more people around the world with two key results: Add 27M new users in 2014; and Reach 80M total registered users. Now, they have over 130M users and are part of the global company Under Armor (UA). However, the transition from a two-man team to their managerial roles at UA were not easy.

Initially, it was straightforward to maintain a to-do-list; however, as they hired more people and grew to supporting 35M users, goal setting became more difficult. It was at this point that their paths crossed with John Doerr. Using the OKR concepts, they were able to focus their teams' efforts. However, even this was not quite enough. A key breakthrough for the brothers was recognizing the need to align the objectives from different parts of the organization.

Key Takeaway: Alignment is about helping people understand what you want them to do.

Following the merger with UA, this lesson again became apparent. They realized that other teams within UA had defined objectives for their team, ones that did not align with their primary OKRs, at least at that point in time. They communicated these OKRs to the other relevant teams, which allowed the other teams to recognize their limits and adjust their requirements appropriately.

Finally, when there is a misalignment with customers' goals and a business goal, they always side with the former. By so doing, they remain connected with the people they serve.

CONNECT: THE INTUIT STORY

Since the 1980s, Intuit has grown and evolved to become one of the "World's Most Admired Companies," according to *Fortune* magazine. Most recently, it sold Quicken (its first product) and developed QuickBooks into an online open platform, resulting in subscriptions that increased by almost 50 percent.

CIO Atticus Tysen introduced the OKR system to the IT group initially to encourage "enthusiastic" and not "bureaucratic" compliance in their process of moving operations to the cloud. In so doing, it demonstrated that OKRs do not have to be rolled out across the entire company but can be tested first in smaller projects.

Intuit's CEO Brad Smith had already started this process by installing a company-wide goal-setting system. Atticus built on this by introducing OKRs.

Key Takeaway: In the so-called cloud era, OKRs can be even more powerful.

One of Intuit's OKR success stories revolved around their collaborations with teams in Bangalore. Being 13 hours away from headquarters, chats, collaborative writing, and videoconferencing were difficult to undertake efficiently. To address this, they elevated a key result related to improving these connections to its own top-level OKR. In six months, they had developed an integrated system that allowed employees to focus on their objectives and not waste time trying to communicate with one another.

OKRs also worked well within Intuit's flat organization. With only a few tiers lying between the CEO and the frontline employees, OKRs opened the IT department horizontally, allowing engineers, for example, to connect directly with one another by linking their objectives together.

SUPERPOWER #3: TRACK FOR ACCOUNTABILITY

Rather than thinking of OKRs as being static, they should be viewed as evolving with a life cycle that includes the setup, shepherding, and tracking.

The setup involves choosing the right framework for capturing the company's OKRs. For a small business, this may simply involve a set of Microsoft Word files, but as the company grows, this system does not provide even basic functionality, such as the ability to search through them for connections and/or alignment. Now, organizations are investing in mobile apps, real-time alerts, and integration with packages such as Zendesk. Together, they increase the visibility of the goals, foster engagement, promote networking, and reduce frustration, whilst saving time and money.

To be effective, an OKR system requires shepherds to guide the flock. These individuals are responsible for enforcing universal adoption of the system.

Like other goal tracking endeavors, OKRs require some metric to assess success. This may be as simple as a weekly check-in to ensure that progress is being made. As part of the tracking progress the owner of the OKR can: (1) continue; (2) update; (3) start; or (4) stop an OKR, depending on the situation.

Key Takeaway: OKRs are living, breathing organisms with three life phases: setup, shepherding, and midlife tracking.

Even when the work associated with the OKR is completed, the OKR can still be analyzed for further insight. Three important aspects are: scoring, subjective self-assessment, and reflection.

Scoring involves giving the OKR a numerical value, say, between zero and one. High values suggest that you delivered, while low values admit that you failed to make much progress. In such a case you might consider whether the objective is still worth pursuing, and, if so, what steps would avoid a similar result.

Self-assessment involves the goal setter's subjective but thoughtful judgment. This can counter-balance scores that may be either too harsh or soft. Either way, they can help facilitate a better process during the next period of performance.

Finally, to avoid the potential "hamster wheel" effect of relentless goal achieving, it is important to pause and reflect on the achievements made, and, in particular, to identify the key lessons from the activities.

THE GATES FOUNDATION STORY

Bill and Melinda Gates formed their eponymous foundation in 2000. Early on, Disability Adjusted Life Years (DALY) provided a data-driven metric for their key results. However, they soon realized that they needed a more structured form of setting goals and investigated OKRs.

Bill Gates had already seen the positive effects of goal-setting from Andy Grove, amongst others, and this, in part, convinced him that OKRs would be a useful concept. In addition to driving success, however, he realized that OKRs could be used to assess failures. One example is the difference between missions and objectives. The former is directional but doesn't include the concrete steps that must be taken to achieve it. While missions can be good, they are not sufficient.

Key Takeaway: OKRs can show when objectives are unachievable allowing you to reallocate resources.

Sometimes, metrics do not measure the right thing. However, by holding themselves accountable, OKR creators can learn from the process and realign their objectives or develop more appropriate metrics to track progress.

The Gates Foundation's most recent top-line objective is to eliminate the parasite causing malaria from the human population. Although challenging, they believe they will succeed, at least in part, because they are employing OKRs.

SUPERPOWER #4: STRETCH FOR AMAZING

OKRs are supposed to push the goal setter out of their comfort zone, allowing them to achieve remarkable results. To accomplish this, however, the goals most be ambitious, that is, they must stretch the person.

Key Takeaway: A "big hairy audacious goal" is one that is both huge and daunting, such as the NASA moon mission.

While it is true that very hard goals are reached much less often than easier goals, there is a strong correlation between the difficulty of the goal and the achievement made. Moreover, the workers who are stretched are more productive, engaged, and motivated.

Google distinguishes between "committed" and "aspirational" goals, with the former being tied to Google's metrics, such as product releases. Aspirational goals, on the other hand reflect higher-risk opportunities. In fact, failure rates of 40 percent are not unusual.

Stretch goals require two elements: They must be important, and people must believe that they are attainable, even if, ultimately, they are not.

It is worth noting that not all advocates of OKRs believe in stretch goals. MyFitnessPal founder, Mike Lee, for example believes that all OKRs should be committed, that is achievable goals. To some extent the balance between the two will depend on the business.

STRETCH: THE GOOGLE CHROME STORY

Google Chrome, a project spearheaded by Sundar Pickai represents a prime example of a stretch goal, and, in fact, even Sundar's career could be a considered a stretch goal. Growing up in South India in the 1980s, in 2015, he became Google's third CEO.

Sundar first implemented and realized the potential of stretch OKRs when he took over management of Google Toolbar, which provided an easy mechanism for searching via Google through another browser.

Google Chrome became a stretch OKR, with the goal of reaching 20 million seven-day active users. Even Sundar secretly didn't think they would be able to achieve this goal in the allotted time, but he didn't convey this to his team. Initially, they struggled to reach just 3 percent penetration, and suffered an additional setback with the Mac version falling significantly behind.

Key Takeaway: Google focuses on speed, striving to make the internet as fast as possible.

Although Google didn't meet their initial goal by 2008, they dug deeper, even using television marketing to explain what browsers do and why Chrome was so much better. In 2009, they set another stretch OKR of 50 million users by the end of the year. They failed again. Ultimately, they set a goal of 111 million users the following year, reaching it by years-end. Today, Chrome resides on over 1 billion users on mobile phones alone.

STRETCH: THE YOUTUBE STORY

In 2014, Susan Wojcicki became the CEO of YouTube and inherited the formidable goal of reaching one billion hours of people watching YouTube every day. This would be a factor of ten increase, and it had to be done within four years.

One of the key revelations for achieving this was to identify and track a better metric. After considering many possibilities, the YouTube team realized that "watch time," not clicks or views was the core metric to be followed. This translates into more advertising, which encourages content creators to make more videos, which, in turn, draws more viewership.

Although one billion hours sounds like a lot, the team reframed it to less than 20 percent of the world's total television watch time. Stated as such, the goal seemed more achievable. With this goal set, the team then experimented with lots of policy decisions to increase watch time.

Key Takeaway: OKRs are particularly useful for fledgling companies just beginning to create their culture.

The one billion hours OKR became YouTube's biggest focus. By early 2016, they appeared to be on track, but as the summer rolled around and people spent more time outside, the numbers dropped. By the autumn though, things were back on track, and they achieved their goal before the year's end.

The one-billion-hour OKR had many other positive benefits, including the need to build out the infrastructure to support it. Also, the team realized that the watch hour metric, while good at the time, may have served its purpose. Currently, they are testing a number of new metrics that incorporate elements of happiness and satisfaction into them.

PART II: THE NEW WORLD OF WORK

CONTINUOUS PERFORMANCE MANAGEMENT: OKRS AND CFRS

Annual performance reviews are expensive and exhausting. In contrast, CFRs (Conversations, Feedback, and Recognition) provide a mechanism for continuous performance management.

Conversations refer to an authentic interaction between manager and employee with the goal of driving better performance.

Feedback consists of two-way communication amongst peers to both assess current progress as well as suggest avenues for future improvement.

Recognition refers to expressions of appreciation to individuals for positive contributions to the business' goals.

CFRs promote transparency, accountability, empowerment, not to mention teamwork. Additionally, they complement OKRs by being mutually reinforcing.

Key Takeaway: Continuous Performance Management includes having conversations, providing feedback, and recognizing deserving people.

The transition from annual reviews to continuous performance management involves several steps. Perhaps the most important being that one must separate raises/bonuses from OKRs; the reason being that the former are backward-looking, while the latter are forward-looking.

CFRs are about connecting with peers and bosses alike. Once a critical mass of people is on board, one person can cheer for another's goal. And, with every cheer, the company moves closer and closer to operating excellence.

DITCHING ANNUAL PERFORMANCE REVIEWS: THE ADOBE STORY

Like many other companies, Adobe held annual performance reviews. However, in 2012, while traveling to India, Donna Morris, an executive with Adobe, vented to a reporter that the company was planning to abolish annual reviews, replacing them with more frequent and forward-facing reviews. Unfortunately, she hadn't yet told Adobe's CEO or her staff about it.

Nevertheless, she began the process to implement it, leading to what became known as "check-in," Adobe's take on continuous performance management.

Key Takeaway: Adobe replaced annual performance reviews with continuous performance management.

At least every six weeks, Adobe contributors get performance feedback that is specific to them. In practice, they receive this feedback on a weekly basis. Constructive, corrective feedback is a key element of this process.

Adobe's system has three components: (1) executive support; (2) alignment with an individual's goals and Adobe's; and (3) investment in training for managers and leaders.

BAKING BETTER EVERY DAY: THE ZUME PIZZA STORY

Zume pizza is a story of David taking on Goliath, and his two big brothers: Domino's, Pizza Hut, and Papa John's. Zume's management began implementing OKRs just days after the first pizzas were delivered.

By combining robotics, artisan and organic pizza, and vans that cook the pizza while on route, they created a unique an irresistible option for those in Silicon Valley.

Key Takeaway: OKRs can be an excellent training tool for managers and leaders.

For the co-CEOs, Julia and Alex, the intrinsic value of OKRs lies in the discipline they enforce on the leaders. They train people to be informed about what is and is not actually possible.

OKRs also provided useful insight even beyond their typical usage. For example, they identified an ambiguity with whose responsibility it was for Zume's revenue targets. Additionally, they serve as a focal point for team building.

The Zume team meet with their direct reports every two weeks. This one-hour meeting cannot be canceled and is treated as sacred. Typically, a meeting with co-CEO Alex might start with: What makes you happy? What saps your energy? How would you describe your dream job? From there, they discuss what his expectations are.

CULTURE

Job seekers today often express a good cultural fit as a top criterion when looking for a job. But how do companies construct and maintain a positive culture? OKRs and CFRs can provide the basis for this by creating alignment between people and their objectives.

A healthy culture can be described by affirmative team answers to a set of questions created by an internal Google study:

- Are the goals, roles, and execution plans clear?

- Can we take risks without feeling embarrassed?

- Are we working on something that's personally important?

- Can we count on each other to meet or exceed their objectives?

- Do we believe that the work really matters?

Key Takeaway: Outstanding performance derives from clear goals, roles, and execution plans.

Coursera, a leading online education system, adopted OKRs in 2013. They connected the OKRs to their values and mission statement, effectively linking it to their culture. By so doing, they have maintained and improved their positive culture across all aspects of the company. Their CEO, Rick Levin couldn't imagine where they would be without OKRs.

Dov Seidman, in his book *HOW: Why HOW We Do Anything Means Everything . . . in Business (and in Life)* proposed that companies will outperform their competition if they "out-behave" them. To achieve this, rules are replaced with shared principles, and their workers are not merely engaged, but inspired. These ideas are linked to OKRs through transparency and connection.

CULTURE CHANGE: THE LUMERIS STORY

Lumeris is a value-based health care organization. Their ultimate goal, as stated by CEO Mike Long, is to "rationalize the nation's health care supply chain" (Doerr, p. 223). He compares it to other industries where success is based on transparent cost, quality, service, and choices. None of this was being relayed to the doctors, because the existing system was opaque.

Wanting to leverage such transparent data, Lumeris looked to OKRs to help them succeed. However, before they could implement them, they first needed to address cultural barriers.

The largest issue was that part of the company was risk averse, while the other part was constantly pushing at the boundaries of what was possible. The net effect was that it was slowing everything down.

Key Takeaway: Culture change can be personal, sometimes propagating at the speed of one conversation at a time.

With positive culture changes in place, the management could now implement OKRs company-wide, with measurable improvements in performance. One unique aspect of their implementation, however, was known as "selling your reds." At their monthly review meetings, rather than focus on the successful OKRs, the team would vote on the most important, but at-risk company-wide OKRs. They would then brainstorm for as long as it took to find ways to bring them back on track.

CULTURE CHANGE: BONO'S ONE CAMPAIGN STORY

Bono launched the ONE campaign in 2004 to facilitate a nonpartisan, grassroots, activist coalition. OKRs were a key ingredient to its success. Moreover, as its objectives have changed from working *on* Africa to working *with* and *in* Africa, OKRs have helped with the transition.

Bono's ONE and DATA non-profit organizations were built around the idea of his hugely successful band, U2, but being more of a punk band—tough opportunists. As great as the work they were doing was, however, it took their first meeting with John Doerr to truly understand who they were working for.

Key Takeaway: If you want to cut a man's hair, it is better if he is in the room (Doerr, p. 239)

Following backlash against Bono's efforts, such as in the book "Dead Aid" by Dambisa Moyo, they realized that their credibility was under threat. Now they are committed to both organizational and cultural change. And OKRs have helped them stay focused on the changes that need to be made.

Bono explains that there is a balance in using OKRs. On one hand, they could stifle the disruptive goals of ONE, particularly if they make ONE become too organized. Plus, you cannot create OKRs that are always successful, you need "red" ones in addition to the "green."

THE GOALS TO COME

The previous chapters have illustrated how OKRs can be implemented in a range of commercial, academic, and non-profit organizations. However, this is merely the beginning. Thus far, OKRs have been considered as simple tools or processes. However, they may become much more.

Thinking of OKRs as a launchpad for the next wave of business adventurers may be more apt. They could have a measurable impact on GDP growth, health care outcomes, government performance, and even social progress. Orly Fiedman, for example, introduced OKRs to every elementary schoolchild at a school in California.

Key Takeaway: Ideas are easy; execution is everything.

By thinking even bigger, we may see the full potential of OKRs. For more information, you can email the author at john@whatmatters.com.

DEDICATION, RESOURCES, AND OTHER CLOSING MATERIAL

The book is dedicated to two extraordinary people: Andy Grove and Bill Campbell.

Resource 1 summarizes Google's OKR playbook. As the largest implementor of OKRs, they have developed a number of key strategies for developing OKRs. This resource summarizes their guidelines and provides some templates.

Resource 2 provides a typical OKR cycle, as might be employed at a company.

Resource 3 provides useful questions for developing performance conversations.

Resource 4 presents a bulleted summary of the key points about OKRs.

Resource 5 provides a number of references for further reading on this, and related topics.

In the acknowledgments, the author thanks the various people who made this book possible.

The author also provides a notes section with many links to additional resources for each chapter.

The book concludes with a detailed index.

EDITORIAL REVIEW

In his book *Measure What Matters*, John Doerr lays out a systematic process for setting objectives with measurable key results that can be implemented within any organization. He also provides a broad range of case studies, narrated by the key people who implemented them. This includes Bill Gates and Larry Page, amongst many others.

The book begins with a brief history of Objectives and Key Results (OKRs), and, in particular, on Andy Grove's impact on Doerr's ideas. He then develops the key attributes of the system, interspersing them with examples for high-profile organizations that he personally advised.

With an engaging writing Style, Doerr demonstrates how OKRs have helped focus organizations and spur them to far greater heights than they would otherwise have been able to reach. The case studies presented span a wide range of disciplines providing useful templates for effectively all types of organizations. Moreover, in a set of indispensable resources at the end of the book, the key elements of the system as well as several templates for implementing them are also provided.

BACKGROUND ON AUTHOR

John Doerr is an engineer, venture capitalist, chairman, and author. For almost 40 years he has helped entrepreneurs build disruptive companies. This unique career made him the only man who could author *Measure What Matters* in 2018. This book, together with his online platform, at WhatMatters.com, provide a distinct and engaging description of OKRs.

Doerr, however, is more than a messenger for this approach. He knows, first-hand, how the process, which was based on a philosophy by Andy Grove of Intel, with whom he worked. He was also an original investor and board member at both Google and Amazon.

Currently, John Doerr serves on the board of the Obama Foundation and ONE.org. He remains passionate about encouraging CEOs and other leaders to consider the impact that OKRs can have on their dreams.

END OF BOOK SUMMARY

*If you enjoyed this **ZIP Reads** publication, we encourage you to purchase a copy of <u>the original book.</u>*

We'd also love an honest review on Amazon.com!

Want *FREE* book summaries delivered weekly? Sign up for our email list and get notified of all our new releases, free promos, and $0.99 deals!

No spam, just books.

Sign up at <u>http://zipreads.co</u>

51623678R00024

Made in the USA
Lexington, KY
05 September 2019